DISCOVER THE
PATHWAY TO WEALTH

A Simple Guide to Financial Freedom and a Happy Life

Dirk R. Lewis

Discover the Pathway to Wealth

A Simple Guide to Financial Freedom and a Happy Life.

Dirk R. Lewis

Copyright © 2023 by Dirk R. Lewis.

All Rights Reserved.

No part of this book may be used or reproduced by any means, graphic, electronic, or mechanical, including photocopying, recording, taping, or by any information storage retrieval system without the written permission of the publisher

<u>Dedication</u>.

I dedicate this book to the world and to all those who seek financial freedom and happiness. May the insights and practical guidance shared within these pages help you discover the pathway to wealth and lead a fulfilling life. And to my beloved family and friends, who have always been my rock and source of motivation, pillars of support, thank you for being my constant source of inspiration.This is dedicated to all of you.

Table of Contents

Chapter 4: Boosting Your Earning Potential

Chapter 5: Investments and Wealth Growth

Your Journey to Financial Freedom

<u>INTRODUCTION</u>

Welcome to a Wealthier and Happier Life

In the bustling tapestry of existence, where dreams and aspirations interweave with the daily grind, we all share a common desire: the pursuit of a wealthier and happier life. It is a universal yearning that transcends borders, cultures, and backgrounds. Whether we envision financial abundance, personal fulfillment, or simply a life lived on our terms, the essence of our pursuit is the same – to find that elusive balance between prosperity and contentment.

At the heart of this journey lies a beacon guiding us towards our desired destination – the beacon of financial freedom. It is the cornerstone upon which our aspirations take shape and the means through which we can transform our dreams into reality. The quest for financial freedom is not merely about accumulating wealth; it is a journey of self-discovery, empowerment, and the ability to lead a life defined by choices rather than constraints.

The Importance of Financial Freedom

Financial freedom is not a mere abstraction; it is the key to unlocking the doors of opportunity, peace of mind, and a sense of security in an unpredictable world. It grants us the ability to pursue our passions, invest in our well-being, and provide for our loved ones without the shackles of financial constraints. It empowers us to weather life's storms, whether they come in the form of unexpected expenses, career changes, or unforeseen challenges.

Imagine a life where the burden of debt is lifted, where work becomes a choice rather than a necessity, and where you can dedicate your time and resources to what truly matters to you. This is the promise of financial freedom, and it is within your reach.

In the pages that follow, we will embark on a journey together – a journey that will demystify the pathways to wealth, happiness, and financial independence. We will explore the principles of sound money management, the art of investing wisely, and the strategies for crafting a life that aligns with your values and aspirations.

But remember, this is not just a book about numbers and investments; it is a guide to building a life of purpose, balance, and joy. It's about equipping you with the knowledge and tools to make informed financial decisions that will shape your future.

So, whether you're starting from scratch, seeking to enhance your financial acumen, or simply looking for inspiration to reignite your wealth-building journey, you've picked up a valuable compass. Welcome to a wealthier and happier life.

Welcome to the pursuit of financial freedom.

Chapter 1: Setting Your Financial Goals

Defining Your Wealth Objectives

Before going on any trip, it's necessary to know your destination. The same approach applies to your financial path toward prosperity and pleasure. To build a path to financial success, you must first identify your wealth goals. These goals will serve as the guiding lights that illuminate your route and help you remain on track, even when confronted with financial storms or diversions along the road.

Your financial goals are not generic; they are very personal and should represent your particular aims, beliefs, and priorities. To establish your financial goals successfully, examine the following steps:

1. Reflect on Your Values:

Take some time to ponder on what is important to you in life. What are your primary beliefs and principles? Your financial objectives should connect with these principles to guarantee that your pursuit of riches is meaningful and enjoyable. For example, if family and education are crucial to you, your financial objectives can include saving for your children's college education or constructing a pleasant house for your family.

2. Determine Your Short-Term and Long-Term Goals:

Divide your financial ambitions into short-term and long-term aims. Short-term objectives often have a timeline of one to three years and may include things like creating an emergency fund, paying off credit card debt, or taking a dream trip. Long-term objectives stretch beyond three years and may cover goals like owning a house, retiring comfortably, or leaving a legacy for future generations.

3. Be Specific and Quantify Your Goals:

Vague objectives are tough to attain because they lack clarity. Instead of stating, "I want to save money," explain how much you want to save and by when. For instance, "I aim to save $10,000 for a down payment on a house within the next two years." Specific and measurable objectives provide you with a clear aim to strive toward.

4. Prioritize Your Goals:

It's crucial to prioritize your financial goals since you may not be able to handle all of them simultaneously. Determine which objectives are most important and match with your current life stage. This will help you arrange your money resources and efforts more efficiently.

5. Consider the SMART Criteria:

Use the SMART criteria to tailor your objectives further. SMART stands for Specific, Measurable, Achievable, Relevant, and Time-bound. When your objectives fit these characteristics, they become more actionable and reachable. For example, a SMART goal would be, "I will save $5,000 for a European vacation within the next 18 months by contributing

$300 per month to a dedicated savings account."

6. Visualize Your Success:

Imagine what accomplishing your financial objectives would look and feel like. Visualization may be a tremendous motivation. Picture yourself debt-free, purchasing your ideal house, or enjoying a comfortable retirement. This mental representation may fuel your drive and help you remain devoted to your aims.

Defining your wealth goals is the essential first step on your road toward financial independence and a happy life. These goals will serve as the basis around which you'll develop your financial strategy and make educated choices. As we advance in this book, we will examine how to develop a thorough financial plan that corresponds with your established objectives, enabling you to walk the route to riches with confidence and purpose.

SMART Goals for Wealth Building

When setting financial goals, it's essential to make them SMART—Specific, Measurable, Achievable, Relevant, and Time-bound. SMART goals provide clarity and structure, making it easier to track your progress and stay motivated on your wealth-building journey. Let's break down each element of SMART goals in the context of wealth building:

1. Specific:

A specific goal is clear and well-defined. Instead of a vague goal like "I want to be rich," specify exactly what you want to achieve. For example, you might set a specific goal to "accumulate $1 million in savings and investments."

2. Measurable:

A measurable goal is quantifiable, allowing you to track your progress objectively. In our example, you can easily measure your progress toward the $1 million goal by checking your savings and investment accounts regularly.

3. Achievable:

An achievable goal is realistic and within reach. While ambitious goals are great, setting an unattainable goal can lead to frustration and disappointment. Assess your current financial situation and determine if your goal is feasible. If your current savings rate and income make it unrealistic to save $1 million in a year, consider extending the timeline to make it achievable.

4. Relevant:

A relevant goal is aligned with your values and long-term objectives. Ensure that your wealth-building goal makes sense in the context of your life. For instance, if you value financial security and early retirement, accumulating a substantial savings nest egg is relevant to your aspirations.

5. Time-bound:

A time-bound goal has a clear deadline. Without a timeframe, your goal lacks urgency, and it's easy to procrastinate. Set a specific date by which you aim to achieve your wealth-building goal. For example, you might decide to accumulate $1 million in savings and investments within 15 years.

Now, let's revisit our SMART goal for wealth building:

SMART Wealth-Building Goal:

"I will collect $1 million in savings and investments during the next 15 years by continuously saving and investing a percentage of my salary each month. I will monitor my progress quarterly to ensure I'm on the correct road. This aim is significant to me since it fits with my desire for financial stability and early retirement."

This SMART goal is precise (accumulating $1 million), measurable (monitoring progress quarterly), attainable (based on a realistic savings strategy), relevant (connected with the aim for financial stability and early retirement), and time-bound (during the next 15 years). It gives a clear path for your wealth-building activities, making it simpler to take concrete measures and remain motivated along the way.

As you work toward your SMART wealth-building objectives, remember that flexibility is also vital. Life may provide unexpected problems or opportunities, and you may need to change your objectives appropriately. Periodically examine and update your financial goals to ensure they stay in tune with your developing financial circumstances and desires.

Chapter 2: understanding money

<u>The Psychology of Money</u>

Money isn't simply a vehicle of transaction; it's a strong force that impacts our ideas, emotions, and actions. To walk the route to wealth effectively, it's vital to grasp the psychology of money—how our attitudes, beliefs, and actions impact our financial results.

1. Money as a Symbol:

Money frequently acts as a metaphor for our goals, aspirations, and concerns. It might indicate security, prosperity, independence, or even pleasure. Understanding what money signifies to you is the first step towards unwinding your connection with it. For others, money implies stability, leading to a cautious attitude to finances. Others consider money as a tool to attain aspirations and are prepared to take calculated risks to fulfill those dreams.

2. Emotions and Money:

Our emotions have a vital impact on financial decision-making. Emotions like fear, greed, and jealousy may lead to hasty and foolish actions. It's vital to understand when emotions are influencing financial choices and acquire techniques to handle them successfully. For example, fear of market volatility could lead to selling assets at the wrong moment, while greed might result in excessive risk-taking.

3. Money Scripts:

We all have money scripts—deep-seated thoughts and attitudes about money sometimes created throughout infancy. These scripts impact our financial actions. Some typical money scripts include "money is the root of all evil," "more money equals more happiness," or "money should be saved, not spent." Identifying your money scripts might help you question and alter them to line better with your financial objectives.

4. Delayed Gratification:

The capacity to defer pleasure is a critical part of financial success. It entails making short-term sacrifices for long-term rewards. Understanding that wealth-building frequently entails delayed pleasure might help you avoid the temptation of impulsive spending and concentrate on your financial ambitions.

5. The Impact of Social Comparison:

Social comparison is a natural propensity to examine our financial condition in relation to others. In today's digital era, it's simpler than ever to compare ourselves to others, which may lead to feelings of inadequacy or a desire for lifestyle inflation. It's crucial to remember that everyone's financial path is unique, and comparison may be unproductive. Focus on your objectives and principles rather than attempting to stay up with others.

6. Overcoming Money Biases:

Cognitive biases, such as confirmation bias and overconfidence, may lead to bad financial choices. Confirmation bias, for example, drives us to seek information that validates our previous opinions while rejecting contrary facts. Being conscious of these biases might help you make more sensible and informed financial decisions.

7. Money and Happiness:

While money may offer stability and provide doors to opportunity, its connection with happiness is complicated. Research demonstrates that after a certain point, more income has decreasing rewards in terms of happiness. Understanding this may help you achieve a balance between pursuing financial objectives and prioritizing other parts of life that contribute to pleasure, such as relationships, health, and personal development.

In this chapter, we've investigated the psychology of money—the ideas, emotions, and behaviors that impact our financial choices. Recognizing the psychological elements at play in your connection with money is the first step toward making more educated, balanced, and empowered financial decisions. As we continue our road to financial independence, we'll dig further into practical ways to use this insight to develop money and create a better, more fulfilled life.

The Importance of Financial Literacy

Financial literacy is the basis upon which prudent financial decision-making and a secure future are constructed. It's not simply a talent; it's a vital life ability that helps folks manage their money efficiently and make educated financial decisions. Here's why financial literacy is of critical importance:

1. Informed Decision-Making:

Financial literacy empowers people with the information and skills to make educated choices about their money. From daily money management to long-term investments, having a strong grasp of financial principles helps individuals to analyze their alternatives and adopt the most suited financial strategy.

2. Avoiding Financial Pitfalls:

Financial illiteracy may lead to expensive errors. Without the capacity to analyze the risks and rewards of diverse financial goods and services, consumers may fall victim to predatory loans, high-interest credit cards, or investment scams that promise fast riches but result in financial devastation. Financial literacy helps individuals identify and avoid these dangers.

3. Achieving Financial Goals:

Whether it's purchasing a house, supporting a child's education, or retiring comfortably, everyone has financial aspirations. Financial literacy is the plan that leads people toward reaching these objectives. It helps individuals to establish realistic targets, construct successful savings and investment programs, and remain on track over the long term.

4. Building Financial Confidence:

Financial literacy builds confidence in handling one's money. When people learn financial fundamentals, they feel more in control of their money. This confidence not only leads to better financial judgments but also decreases stress and anxiety associated with money concerns.

5. Navigating Life Transitions:

Life is full of adjustments, such as establishing a family, changing employment, or confronting unanticipated crises. Financial literacy prepares people to negotiate these changes with more ease. They may alter their financial strategies to fit changing circumstances and make educated decisions throughout crucial life events.

6. Enhancing Economic Well-Being:

A financially knowledgeable person helps with overall economic stability. When individuals make solid financial choices, they are less likely to depend on social safety nets, and they may contribute constructively to the economy via saving, investing, and responsible spending.

7. Empowerment and Independence:

Financial literacy helps people to take control of their financial fate. It minimizes dependency on financial consultants or institutions, offering consumers the tools they need to handle their money independently. This attitude of empowerment develops self-reliance and autonomy.

8. Teaching the Next Generation:

Financial knowledge is a gift that may be handed down through generations. When parents or caregivers are financially educated, they may teach their children basic money management skills. This not only helps the present generation but also lays the way for a financially responsible future.

In today's complicated financial market, where options concerning savings, investments, mortgages, and retirement plans are numerous, financial literacy is more vital than ever. It's a lifelong learning process that grows with shifting financial conditions and ambitions. As we advance in this book, you'll obtain the information and skills required to strengthen your financial literacy and utilize it as a strong advantage in your quest for prosperity and happiness.

Chapter 3: Building a Solid Financial Foundation

Budgeting and Money Management

One of the pillars of financial success and a secure financial future is smart budgeting and money management. Your financial foundation starts with the way you handle the money you make. In this chapter, we will cover the significance of budgeting and money management, along with practical ways to help you develop a sound financial platform.

Understanding Budgeting:

A budget is a financial plan that details your income and spending. It acts as a blueprint for your financial life, helping you utilize your resources properly and accomplish your financial objectives. Here's why budgeting is so crucial:

1. Control Over Your Finances:

Budgeting offers you control over your money rather than allowing your money dominate you. It helps you to understand where your money is going and make deliberate choices about how to utilize it.

2. Financial Awareness:

Creating a budget requires you to be conscious of your financial status. You'll know precisely how much you're making, how much you're spending, and where your money is going. This knowledge is the first step in making substantial financial improvements.

3. Goal Achievement:

Budgets are not simply about monitoring costs; they are a tool for reaching your financial objectives. Whether it's saving for a down payment on a home, paying off debt, or going on a dream trip, a well-structured budget may help you allocate finances toward these goals.

4. Emergency Preparedness:

Budgeting involves saving away cash for emergencies or unexpected costs. This financial cushion may give peace of mind and shield you from financial misfortunes.

Practical Steps for Effective Budgeting and Money Management:

1) Income Assessment:

Start by estimating your entire monthly revenue, including your salary, side hustles, rental income, and any other sources of money.

2) Expense Tracking:

Track your spending for at least a month. Categorize your expenditure into necessary categories (e.g., housing, utilities, food) and discretionary categories (e.g., entertainment, eating out).

3) Create a Budget:

Based on your income and spending monitoring, build a budget. Allocate a part of your income to each spending area, including savings and debt payments.

4) Set Financial Goals:

Determine your short-term and long-term financial objectives. Your budget should contain provisions for saving and investing to attain these objectives.

5) Prioritize Saving:

Make saving a non-negotiable element of your budget. Set up automatic payments to your savings or investing accounts to maintain regularity.

6) Reduce Discretionary Spending:

Identify places where you can decrease discretionary expenditure. This might mean eating out less, lowering entertainment spending, or finding more cost-effective alternatives.

7) Emergency Fund:

Aim to develop an emergency fund that covers at least three to six months' worth of living costs. This fund offers a financial safety net in case of unforeseen circumstances.

8) Debt Management:

Create a strategy to pay off high-interest debt methodically. Allocate additional dollars from your budget to hasten debt payback.

9) Regular Review:

Review your budget periodically, ideally monthly, to verify you're remaining on target. Adjust your budget as required to meet changes in your financial condition or aspirations.

10) Seek Professional Advice:

If you're dealing with debt or difficult financial concerns, consider receiving guidance from a financial expert or counselor. They can give specialized counsel to help you manage your money properly.

Budgeting and money management may take discipline and care, but they are key components of having a good financial foundation. By following these practical steps and making budgeting a continuous part of your daily routine, you'll not only gain control over your money but also pave the road for accomplishing your financial objectives and ensuring your future.

Emergency Funds and Rainy-Day Savings for Financial Freedom

In the path towards financial independence and stability, the necessity of having emergency cash and rainy-day savings cannot be emphasized. These financial cushions operate as a safety net, giving you with the peace of mind and resilience required to weather unanticipated storms while preserving your long-term financial objectives. Let's discuss why emergency money and rainy-day savings are vital components of your financial plan.

1. Financial Stability and Peace of Mind:

Life is unpredictable, and unforeseen bills might develop at any time. Whether it's a medical emergency, a vehicle repair, or an unexpected job loss, having a well-funded emergency fund guarantees that you can manage these unanticipated financial obstacles without derailing your entire financial strategy. This stability contributes to peace of mind and less financial stress.

2. Avoiding Debt Accumulation:

When crises arise and you don't have adequate resources to handle them, the temptation to depend on credit cards or loans might be powerful. This may lead to debt buildup and interest payments that cut into your financial resources. A well-established emergency fund helps you escape this financial trap.

3. Continuity of Financial Goals:

Financial independence frequently requires identifying and attaining particular objectives, such as purchasing a property, retiring comfortably, or starting a company. Without emergency reserves, unanticipated costs might move your resources away from these goals.

Rainy-day funds guarantee that your long-term financial objectives stay on track, regardless of short-term financial setbacks.

4. Avoiding Financial Crises:

In times of financial difficulty, such as a recession or economic slump, having emergency cash offers a necessary safety net. It helps you to meet critical costs and maintain your lifestyle while pursuing new earning prospects or waiting for a favorable financial environment.

5. Reducing Emotional Stress:

Financial crises may be emotionally demanding. They impair your feeling of security and well-being. Knowing that you have a financial cushion in place helps you to concentrate on finding solutions to the issue rather than stressing about how to fund current costs.

6. Building Financial Resilience:

Financial resilience is the capacity to bounce back from financial losses. Emergency reserves and rainy-day savings are the cornerstone of this resiliency. They help you to withstand shocks and continue your financial path with minimum disturbance.

How to Build and Maintain Emergency Funds and Rainy-Day Savings:

1) Set Savings Goals:

Determine how much you need in your emergency fund and rainy-day reserves. A usual suggestion is to plan for three to six months' worth of living costs in your emergency fund plus an extra fund for minor, unforeseen emergencies.

2) Create a Separate Account:

Open separate savings accounts for your emergency fund and rainy-day funds. This distinction helps you avoid spending these monies on non-emergencies.

3) Consistent Saving:

Make saving a regular component of your financial regimen. Set up automatic payments from your primary account to your emergency fund and rainy-day reserves.

4) Emergency Fund First:

Prioritize establishing your emergency savings before concentrating on other financial objectives. Having this money in place offers a necessary safety net.

5) Regularly Replenish:

If you dip into your emergency fund or rainy-day savings for a true emergency, make it a point to restore them as quickly as possible.

6) Review and Adjust:

Periodically assess the goal amounts for your emergency fund and rainy-day reserves. As your financial condition changes, you may need to revise these objectives.

7) Avoid Temptations:

Reserve these cash strictly for actual emergencies and unforeseen needs. Avoid utilizing them for frivolous expenditures or non-essential goods.

8) Seek Professional Advice:

If you're confused about how much to save or how to distribute your money across various funds, consider seeing a financial counselor. They may give individualized assistance based on your unique circumstances and aspirations.

Emergency reserves and rainy-day savings are not luxuries; they are financial needs. They give the stability and flexibility you need to overcome life's challenges while achieving long-term financial independence. By rigorously creating and maintaining these financial buffers, you'll improve your financial foundation and position yourself for greater resilience

and success on your journey to financial
independence.

Managing Debt Wisely to Build a Solid Financial Foundation.

Debt may be a double-edged sword on your journey to financial independence. When handled effectively, debt may be a beneficial instrument for accomplishing financial objectives. However, if left unchecked, it may become a substantial hurdle to your financial stability and freedom. Here, we'll study the tactics for managing debt responsibly to develop a strong financial foundation on your route to financial independence.

1. Understand Your Debt:

The first step in managing debt effectively is to comprehend it thoroughly. This involves understanding the kinds of debt you have (e.g., student loans, credit card debt, mortgage) and the conditions of each loan (e.g., interest rates, repayment schedules). Understanding the intricacies of your debt helps you make educated choices.

2. Prioritize High-Interest Debt:

Not all loans are created equal. High-interest loans, such as credit card debt, often have higher interest rates and may swiftly undermine your financial health. Make paying off high-interest bills a priority. Allocate as much additional money as feasible toward these obligations to decrease interest payments.

3. Create a Debt Repayment Plan:

Develop a comprehensive debt payback strategy that describes how you'll approach each loan. You could opt to employ the avalanche approach (paying off the highest interest rate debt first) or the snowball method (paying off the smallest debt first for rapid victories). Stick to your selected plan continuously.

4. Budget for Debt Repayment:

Incorporate debt payback into your monthly budget. Allocate a particular amount of your income toward paying off debt. Treating debt repayment as a monthly cost guarantees that you continually make progress toward being debt-free.

5. Avoid New Debt:

While paying off current debt, avoid accruing additional debt. Be careful of your spending patterns and the temptation to utilize credit for non-essential goods. Cut up credit cards if required to avoid impulsive spending.

6. Negotiate Better Terms:

If you have high-interest loans or credit card debt, try negotiating with your creditors for better terms. This might involve asking lower interest rates, reducing fees, or extending repayment schedules to minimize monthly payments.

7. Build an Emergency Fund:

Simultaneously, focus on accumulating an emergency fund, as indicated before. Having an emergency fund means that you may meet unforeseen needs without turning to high-interest loans, lowering financial stress.

8. Explore Debt Consolidation:

Debt consolidation is consolidating various loans into a single, more manageable loan with a reduced interest rate. It may simplify your debt repayment efforts and minimize the overall interest you pay. However, be careful and explore your alternatives fully, since not all consolidation offers are favorable.

9. Seek Professional Advice:

If your debt situation is complicated or burdensome, consider receiving guidance from a financial counselor or expert. They can give assistance on debt management tactics and help you investigate choices like debt consolidation or negotiation.

10. Celebrate Milestones:

As you make progress in paying off debt, celebrate your accomplishments. Whether it's paying off a credit card, a vehicle loan, or a college loan, appreciating your successes may drive you to remain on track and continue your road toward financial independence.

Managing debt sensibly is a vital component of creating a good financial foundation. By taking charge of your debt, setting a smart repayment plan, and making continuous efforts to decrease and eliminate high-interest debt, you'll free up more of your income for savings

and investments. This smart approach to
debt management will eventually speed
your journey toward financial
independence and stability.

Part II: Income and Wealth Creation

Chapter 4: Boosting Your Earning Potential

<u>Career Advancement Strategies</u>

Your work is not only a source of money; it's a key aspect in your route to financial independence. Maximizing your earning potential is a critical component of developing money and attaining your financial objectives. In this chapter, we'll discuss professional growth ideas to assist you boost your income and better your financial prospects.

1. Continuous Learning and Skill Development:

Investing in your abilities and knowledge is one of the most effective methods to progress in your profession. Stay up-to-date with industry trends and innovations. Consider taking classes, attending seminars, or obtaining credentials that are relevant to your profession. The more valuable your skill set, the more you may charge in terms of salary.

2. Set Clear Career Goals:

Define your professional goals and objectives. Where do you see yourself in one year, five years, or 10 years? Having defined objectives offers direction and drive. It helps you make smart choices about your professional path and the abilities you need to acquire.

3. Networking and Building Relationships:

Networking is a vital component of job growth. Building professional connections may lead to new possibilities, mentoring, and useful insights. Attend industry conferences, join relevant organizations, and engage with people both within and beyond your firm.

4. Seek Mentorship and Guidance:

Mentorship is a crucial resource for professional success. Identify seasoned people in your sector who can give direction and help. A mentor can help you manage problems, make educated professional choices, and share their expertise and experience.

5. Take Initiative:

Proactive people generally stand out in their jobs. Look for methods to take on extra responsibility, offer new initiatives, or make changes in your workplace. Taking initiative indicates your devotion and leadership potential.

6. Showcase Your Achievements:

Don't be bashful in highlighting your successes. Keep a record of your successes, such as successful projects, better procedures, or cost-saving efforts. These accomplishments might be important when bargaining for increases or promotions.

7. Effective Communication:

Strong communication skills are vital in every industry. Whether it's presenting ideas, making reports, or cooperating with coworkers, good communication may set you apart. Consider attending seminars or workshops to enhance your communication skills if required.

8. Seek Feedback and Self-Improvement:

Feedback is a useful tool for personal and professional improvement. Solicit feedback from bosses, coworkers, or mentors, and utilize it constructively to enhance your performance. Self-awareness and a dedication to

self-improvement are important to job
progress.

9. Consider Further Education:

Depending on your sector, extra
education, such as a master's degree or
advanced certifications, may considerably
enhance your earning potential. Evaluate
if more education matches with your
professional objectives and industry
criteria.

10. Negotiate Compensation
Thoughtfully:

When discussing salary, approach talks
wisely and boldly. Research industry
compensation standards and be prepared
to justify your worth to the firm. Don't be
scared to ask for what you feel you're
worth.

11. Explore New Opportunities:

Periodically examine your career trajectory and determine if new work prospects correspond better with your objectives and financial desires. Be open to investigating alternative positions, sectors, or geographic areas if it might lead to professional progress.

12. Work-Life Balance:

Achieving job development doesn't imply abandoning work-life balance. A well-balanced life adds to general well-being and work happiness, which may, in turn, increase your performance and development prospects.

Career Progression.

Career progression is a dynamic process that involves continual work and adaptation. By applying these career progression tactics, you'll not only enhance your earning potential but also position yourself for long-term financial success. Remember that your profession is a crucial asset on your route to financial independence, and preemptive efforts may help you utilize it successfully.

Boosting Your Earning Potential: Exploring Multiple Income Streams

In today's changing market, depending simply on a single source of income may not be enough to meet your financial objectives and acquire the amount of financial independence you seek. One smart technique for boosting your earning potential is to study and build various revenue sources. Diversifying your revenue sources not only gives more financial security but also opens new prospects for wealth-building. In this chapter, we'll look into the notion of various revenue streams and how to build and manage them successfully.

Understanding Multiple Income Streams:

Multiple income streams relate to the technique of producing revenue from numerous sources, outside your principal employment or vocation. These extra streams may come from different channels, including side jobs, investments, passive income sources, and more. The objective is to establish a more solid financial foundation that can survive economic swings and help you attain financial independence sooner.

Benefits of Multiple Income Streams:

1) Financial Security: Having various income sources may offer a safety net in case one source of income is disturbed, such as job loss or a decrease in hours.

This financial stability may ease stress during hard times.

2) Accelerated Savings: Additional income sources may greatly enhance your savings rate, helping you to attain your objectives quicker, whether it's paying off debt, establishing an emergency fund, or investing for retirement.

3) Wealth Building: Multiple revenue sources give the ability to acquire wealth more rapidly. With extra income from multiple sources, you may invest in assets that increase over time, such as stocks, real estate, or enterprises.

4) Diverse Skill growth: Exploring numerous revenue sources typically means obtaining new skills and information, which may increase your overall professional and personal growth.

5) Increased Financial Freedom: As your revenue sources develop, you get more

control over your financial life. You become less dependent on a single employment or income, leading to improved financial independence and flexibility.

Exploring and Managing Multiple Income Streams:

1) Identify Your Skills and Interests:

Start by recognizing your skills, abilities, and hobbies that might possibly create revenue. Are you competent in writing, graphic design, programming, or teaching? Recognizing your talents is the first step.

2)Research Income Opportunities:

Investigate numerous revenue sources relevant to your talents and hobbies. This might involve freelancing, consulting, tutoring, or launching a small company.

Research possible markets and demand for your services.

3) Time Management:

Balancing numerous revenue sources needs excellent time management. Create a timetable that enables you to commit dedicated time to each revenue stream while keeping a good work-life balance.

4) Financial Planning:

Develop a financial plan that specifies how you will distribute revenue from each source. Prioritize savings, investments, and debt reduction to line with your financial objectives.

5) Stay Adaptable:

Be open to new chances and adjust as circumstances change. The landscape of employment and income prospects is constantly, so being adaptable and prepared to pivot is key.

6) Tax Considerations:

Understand the tax consequences of different income sources. Consult with a tax adviser to ensure you're managing your revenue streams in a tax-efficient way.

7) Monitor and Evaluate:

Regularly examine the performance of each revenue source. Are there ways to improve revenue or simplify operations? Continuous monitoring ensures that your efforts stay successful.

8) Invest for Passive Income:

Explore passive income sources, such as dividend-paying equities, rental properties, or royalties from intellectual property. Passive income needs less active effort and might bring continuous financial rewards.

8) Risk Management:

Diversify your revenue sources to spread risk. Relying too much on a single source might leave you exposed. A broad income portfolio might give better stability.

9) Plan for Retirement:

Consider how your different revenue sources will support your retirement objectives. Continue contributing to retirement accounts and examine other retirement savings choices for self-employed persons.

Creating and maintaining several income sources requires time and devotion, but the returns may be enormous. As you diversify your income sources, you not only enhance your earning potential but also strengthen your financial foundation,

making you more equipped to reach your
financial objectives and acquire the
financial independence you seek.

Chapter 5: Investments and Wealth Growth

Investing Basics

Investing is a fundamental component of developing wealth and obtaining financial independence. It entails putting your money to work with the purpose of earning a return or profit over time. In this chapter, we'll discuss the foundations of investing, including why it's vital, various sorts of investments, and critical ideas to bear in mind as you begin on your investment journey.

Why Investing Matters

Investing plays a key part in your financial path for various reasons:

1) Wealth Building: Investments have the ability to expand your wealth over time, frequently at a rate that outpaces

inflation. This development may help you reach long-term financial objectives, including as retirement or purchasing a house.

2) Income Generation: Many assets, such as dividend-paying stocks or rental properties, may offer a continuous stream of income, supplementing your principal source of revenue.

3) Diversification: Investing helps you to diversify your financial portfolio. Diversification distributes risk across several asset classes, lessening the effect of poor performance in any one sector.

4) Inflation Hedge: Investing in assets that increase in value helps safeguard your buying power against inflation, ensuring that your money keeps its true worth over time.

Types of Investments

There are several investing alternatives accessible, each with its unique risk and return profile. Here are some popular forms of investments:

1) Stocks: When you acquire a share of stock, you own a piece of a corporation. Stocks offer the potential for large gains but also come with more volatility and risk.

2) Bonds: Bonds are debt instruments issued by governments, businesses, or municipalities. They make monthly interest payments and refund the principle amount at maturity, making them substantially less risky than equities.

3) Real Estate: Real estate investments entail purchasing properties for rental revenue or capital gain. Real estate may

offer a consistent revenue stream and substantial tax advantages.

4) Mutual Funds: Mutual funds combine money from different participants to invest in a broad portfolio of stocks, bonds, or other assets. They provide variety and skilled management.

5) Exchange-Traded Funds (ETFs): ETFs are comparable to mutual funds but trade on stock markets like individual equities. They offer variety and are noted for their low expenditure ratios.

6) Retirement Accounts: Retirement accounts, such as 401(k)s or IRAs, provide tax benefits for long-term investment. They may involve a number of investing possibilities.

8) Savings and Money Market Accounts: These low-risk solutions give a secure location to deposit money and earn

minimal return. They are excellent for short-term aims or emergency finances.

Investment Principles

As you begin on your financial path, keep these key ideas in mind:

1) Diversification: Spread your assets among multiple asset types (stocks, bonds, real estate, etc.) to lessen risk.

2) Risk Tolerance: Assess your risk tolerance and pick assets that fit with your comfort level. Riskier investments may provide larger potential profits but come with more volatility.

3) Time Horizon: Consider your investing time horizon. Longer time horizons may withstand greater risk and may benefit from compounding rewards.

4) Expenses and Fees: Be careful of investment expenses and fees, such as management fees or trading charges. Lower-cost investments may have a substantial influence on your total results.

5) Research and Education: Continuously educate yourself about various investments and tactics. Knowledge is a crucial tool for making educated financial choices.

6) Stay Informed: Keep up with market news and economic events, but avoid making hasty judgments based on short-term changes.

7) Set Clear Goals: Define your financial goals and objectives. Your investing approach should match with these aims.

8) Regular Monitoring: Periodically check your financial portfolio to ensure it stays in line with your objectives and risk tolerance. Rebalance if required.

9) Long-Term Perspective: Investing is often a long-term activity. Avoid making knee-jerk responses to market volatility and concentrate on your long-term aims.

Investing is a strong instrument for wealth creation, but it comes with inherent dangers. The trick is to approach it with meticulous preparation, a diverse portfolio, and a long-term view. By knowing the fundamentals of investing and adhering to strong investment practices, you may work toward creating a solid financial foundation and attaining your financial objectives.

Diversifying Your Investment Portfolio for Wealth Growth

Diversification is a key approach for attaining wealth development while controlling risk in your investing portfolio. The premise of diversification is simple: instead of placing all your eggs in one basket, diversify your assets among several asset classes and securities. This method helps to limit the effect of poor performance in any particular investment and gives a more steady and possibly better return on your whole portfolio. Here's why diversity is vital for wealth creation and how to apply it effectively:

1) Minimizing Risk:

One of the key advantages of diversity is risk reduction. Different sorts of investments have varied amounts of risk, and they don't all go in the same direction at the same time. When you own a variety of assets in your portfolio, it's less likely that a loss in one item would badly harm your overall portfolio. This mitigates the risk of losing a major amount of your capital due to poor performance in a single asset or asset class.

2) Enhancing Returns:

Diversification might possibly boost your total profits. While certain assets may fail in a particular time, others may succeed. By keeping a diverse portfolio, you have the ability to profit from good results while cushioning the effect of bad ones. Over the long run, this may contribute to more constant wealth growth.

3) Achieving Financial Goals:

Different investments are suitable to different financial objectives and time periods. For example, equities may be excellent for long-term wealth development, while bonds give stability and income. By diversifying your assets according to your financial objectives, you're better positioned to attain those goals on time.

How to Diversify Effectively:

1) Asset Classes: Diversify among key asset classes, including equities, bonds, real estate, and cash or cash equivalents. Each asset class has a risk-return profile, and combining them can help balance risk and possible profit.

2) Geographic Diversification: Invest in assets from diverse locations and marketplaces. Global diversity may lessen risks connected with country-specific economic variables and geopolitical events.

3) Industry and Sector Diversification: Within each asset class, distribute your assets across multiple industries and

sectors. This decreases the risk associated with the underperformance of a specific.

4) Individual Securities: If investing in stocks or bonds, consider owning a diversified variety of individual securities rather than concentrating your assets on a few firms or issuers. This lessens the effect of bad performance by a single unit.

5) Investment Vehicles: Utilize a variety of investment vehicles, including mutual funds, exchange-traded funds (ETFs), and individual equities. Investment vehicles like mutual funds and ETFs frequently offer built-in diversity by combining money from numerous participants.

6) Risk Tolerance: Assess your risk tolerance and adapt your diversification plan properly. If you have a greater risk tolerance, you may devote a bigger

amount of your portfolio to stocks and real estate. If you have a reduced risk tolerance, you may select bonds and cash equivalents.

7) Regular Rebalancing: Periodically assess your portfolio to ensure that it stays diversified according to your goal allocation. Rebalance by purchasing or selling assets as required to put your portfolio back in line with your aims.

8) Long-Term Perspective: Diversification is most successful when seen through a long-term viewpoint. Avoid the temptation to make frequent adjustments to your portfolio based on short-term market volatility.

Remember that diversification does not remove risk totally but helps manage and spread it. It's vital to periodically examine and alter your diversification plan as your financial objectives, risk tolerance, and market circumstances change. By adopting a well-thought-out diversification plan, you may boost the potential for wealth creation while decreasing the effect of market volatility on your entire portfolio.

Long-Term Wealth Building for Investment and Wealth Growth

Building large wealth over the long term is a goal that involves a mix of disciplined saving, savvy investment, and patience. Whether you aim to retire comfortably, attain financial independence, or leave a lasting financial legacy, long-term wealth building is a path that may lead to financial stability and peace of mind. Here are fundamental ideas and tactics for successful long-term wealth growth via investing:

1. Start Early and Be Consistent:

The strength of compounding makes beginning early one of the most crucial variables in long-term wealth creation. Compounding permits your assets to earn returns on both your original cash and the reinvested profits. The sooner you begin, the more time your assets have to develop. Be consistent in your savings and investing contributions, even if they start modest. Consistency is crucial to harnessing the power of compounding.

2. Set Clear Financial Goals:

Define your financial objectives, both short-term and long-term. Having precise goals helps you remain focused and motivated. Your objectives can include retirement planning, purchasing a house, supporting your children's education, or obtaining a specific level of wealth. Each objective may demand a different investing approach and time range.

3. Risk Tolerance and Asset Allocation:
Assess your risk tolerance and build an asset allocation plan that corresponds with your risk tolerance and financial

objectives. A well-diversified portfolio that contains a mix of assets including stocks, bonds, real estate, and cash equivalents may help balance risk and possible profit. Adjust your asset allocation as your objectives and risk tolerance vary over time.

4. Embrace Long-Term Thinking:

Successful long-term wealth creation demands patience and a focus on the larger picture. Avoid the temptation to seek short-term profits or make rash investing choices based on market swings. Short-term volatility is a common element of investing, and a long-term perspective helps you ride through market downturns.

5. Regularly Contribute and Reinvest:

Consistently contribute to your financial portfolio, whether via monthly payments to retirement accounts, automated transfers to brokerage accounts, or other ways. Reinvest dividends, interest, and capital gains to optimize the compounding impact. Regular contributions and investments boost wealth accumulation over time.

6. Diversification and Risk Management:

Diversify your assets to disperse risk across numerous asset classes and individual equities. Diversification lessens the effect of poor performance in any particular investment. Maintain an emergency reserve to meet unforeseen needs, so you don't need to sell assets early in situations.

7. Tax-Efficient Strategies:

Consider tax-efficient measures including investing in tax-advantaged retirement accounts (e.g., 401(k)s, IRAs) and employing tax-efficient investment vehicles. Tax-efficient investment may help you retain more of your earnings and limit the effect of taxes on your wealth development.

8. Review and Adjust:

Regularly assess your investing portfolio to ensure it is aligned with your objectives and risk tolerance. Periodically rebalance your portfolio to bring it back to your intended asset allocation. Adjust your financial strategy if your life circumstances change.

9. Seek Professional Guidance:

If you're confused about investing options, consider seeing a financial professional or planner. They may give specialized assistance and help you design a long-term wealth-building plan geared to your unique requirements and objectives.

10. Stay Informed and Educated:

The investing landscape develops, and remaining educated about market trends, economic developments, and investment possibilities is crucial. Continue to educate yourself and alter your investing approach as required.

Long-term wealth creation is not a one-size-fits-all activity. Your plan should be personalized to your individual financial condition, goals, and risk tolerance. By constantly following these rules and changing your strategy as required, you may work towards generating considerable wealth over the long term, accomplishing your financial objectives, and protecting your financial future

Part III: Financial Planning and Management

Chapter 6: Retirement Planning

<u>The Importance of Retirement Savings</u>

Retirement is a big life milestone that demands cautious financial preparation. It's the era when you move from working life to enjoying the results of your effort and following your hobbies and goals. The cornerstone of a safe and enjoyable retirement is a solid retirement savings strategy. In this chapter, we'll underline the vital necessity of retirement savings and why it should be a priority in your financial path.

1. Financial Independence:

Retirement savings serve as the major way of gaining financial independence in your later years. Without appropriate savings, you may find yourself depending on restricted social security payments or suffering financial difficulties throughout retirement.

2. Maintaining Your Lifestyle:

Retirement enables you to pursue the lifestyle you wish without the pressure of work-related commitments. To maintain your pre-retirement quality of life, you'll need adequate money to pay your costs, including housing, healthcare, leisure activities, and travel.

3. Inflation Protection:

Over time, the cost of living tends to grow owing to inflation. Retirement savings can shield you from the eroding impacts of inflation by providing a pool of assets that may produce income and increase in value, ensuring that your spending power stays intact.

4. Healthcare Costs:

As you age, healthcare expenditures tend to grow. Having a solid retirement savings plan may assist meet medical bills, including insurance premiums, co-pays, and long-term care, without draining your assets.

5. Peace of Mind:

Retirement may be a moment of leisure and introspection, free from the stress of work-related responsibilities. Adequate retirement savings give peace of mind, knowing that you have the financial means to fulfill your demands and manage unforeseen costs throughout your retirement years.

6. Flexible Retirement Timing:

Having considerable retirement assets offers you the opportunity to choose when and how you retire. You may retire sooner if desired or continue working part-time if you like your job or prefer to explore a new professional path during your retirement years.

7. Legacy and Family Support:

Retirement savings might also act as a legacy for your loved ones or a tool to help family members in times of need. It might offer a financial buffer for your heirs or enable you to make a lasting influence via charitable gifts.

8. Reducing Financial Stress:

A lack of retirement funds may lead to financial stress throughout retirement,

harming your physical and emotional
well-being. By saving regularly and
developing a solid retirement fund, you
may decrease the worry associated with
financial uncertainty in your elder years.

9. Avoiding Dependence on Others:

Having your retirement funds means that
you may preserve your financial freedom
and avoid being a financial burden on
your family or loved ones. It enables you
to enjoy your retirement on your terms.

10. Maximizing Your Retirement
Experience:

Ultimately, retirement is a time to pursue
new interests, activities, and experiences.
A well-funded retirement savings plan
helps you to optimize your retirement
experience by enabling you to follow your

hobbies and accomplish your long-held aspirations.

The significance of retirement savings cannot be emphasized. To have a happy and secure retirement, it's necessary to start saving early, continuously contribute to your retirement accounts, and invest properly. As you develop in your profession and life, occasionally evaluate your retirement objectives and change your savings plan to ensure that you are on track to reach the retirement you desire. Planning and conscientious saving now will prepare the road for a joyful and financially sound retirement tomorrow.

Retirement Account Options

Retirement accounts are a cornerstone of long-term financial planning, delivering tax benefits and specific features intended to help you prepare for retirement. Choosing the correct retirement accounts and maximizing your contributions are crucial stages in guaranteeing a pleasant retirement. Here, we'll review some of the most prevalent retirement account alternatives accessible to people in the United States.

1. 401(k) Plans:

Employer-Sponsored: Many firms provide 401(k) plans as part of their employee benefits package. These plans let you to contribute a percentage of your paycheck to a tax-deferred retirement account. Employers may also give matching contributions, thus increasing your savings.

Traditional vs. Roth: Traditional 401(k) contributions are made using pre-tax monies, decreasing your taxable income for the year. Roth 401(k) contributions are made using after-tax monies, but withdrawals in retirement are tax-free.

Contribution limitations: Contribution limitations for 401(k) plans are subject to periodic revisions. As of my latest knowledge update in September 2021, the annual contribution ceiling for a 401(k) was $19,500, with an extra $6,500 catch-up contribution for persons aged 50 or older.

2. Individual Retirement Accounts (IRAs):

Traditional IRA: Contributions to a traditional IRA may be tax-deductible, decreasing your taxable income in the year of the contribution. Earnings in the account grow tax-deferred, while withdrawals in retirement are subject to income tax.

Roth IRA: Roth IRAs offer after-tax contributions, so you won't earn a tax deduction when you contribute. However, eligible withdrawals, including wages, are totally tax-free in retirement.

Contribution Limits: As of September 2021, the annual contribution maximum for IRAs was $6,000, with a $1,000 catch-up contribution for those aged 50 or older.

3. SEP IRAs and SIMPLE IRAs:

SEP IRA (Simplified Employee Pension IRA): SEP IRAs are meant for small company owners and self-employed people. Contributions are tax-deductible, and companies contribute on behalf of qualifying workers.

SIMPLE IRA (Savings Incentive Match Plan for Employees): SIMPLE IRAs are also for small enterprises. Employers must make payments, and workers may make contributions via wage deferrals. Contributions are tax-deductible.

4. Self-Employed 401(k) or Solo 401(k):

Designed for self-employed persons or small company owners with no workers (save a spouse), a solo 401(k) lets you to make both employee and employer contributions. This may be a strong retirement savings strategy for self-employed persons.
5. Health Savings Account (HSA):

While mainly utilized for healthcare bills, HSAs may function as a great retirement savings vehicle. Contributions are tax-deductible, gains grow tax-free, and withdrawals for eligible medical costs are tax-free. After age 65, you may withdraw money for non-medical costs without penalties (but income tax may apply).

6. Thrift Savings Plan (TSP):

TSPs are retirement programs for government workers and members of the uniformed forces. Contributions may be made on a pre-tax or Roth basis, and the government may match contributions in certain situations.

7. Pension Plans:

Some firms provide defined benefit pension plans, which give workers with a set retirement income based on pay and years of service. These programs are less frequent now than in the past but still exist in certain sectors.

8. 457 Plans:

Government and some non-profit businesses provide 457 plans, which are comparable to 401(k) plans but with certain distinct characteristics. Contributions may lower taxable income, and withdrawals are normally permitted without penalty following separation from service.

Choosing the correct retirement accounts relies on your specific circumstances, including your job condition, income level, and financial objectives. It's essential to contact with a financial adviser or tax specialist to discover the most suited retirement account alternatives for your retirement planning goals. Additionally, frequently examine and adapt your retirement contributions and investment plan as your financial position develops and retirement objectives change over time.

Chapter 7: Tax Strategies

Tax-Efficient Investing

When developing and maintaining your investment portfolio, it's crucial to consider the effect of taxes. Taxes may considerably impact your investment returns, so implementing tax-efficient investing techniques might help you retain more of your hard-earned money. In this chapter, we'll study tax-efficient investing and share ideas on how to maximize your assets for tax benefits.

1. Choose Tax-Advantaged Accounts:

One of the most efficient strategies to reduce the tax impact on your assets is to utilize tax-advantaged accounts, such as Individual Retirement Accounts (IRAs), 401(k)s, Health Savings Accounts (HSAs), and 529 college savings programs. These accounts provide varied tax advantages, including tax-deductible contributions, tax-deferred growth, or tax-free withdrawals, depending on the account type and your circumstances.

2. Asset Location Strategy:

Asset placement includes carefully arranging different kinds of assets in various account types to improve tax efficiency. Generally, it's best to keep tax-inefficient assets, such as actively managed funds with high turnover or bonds with frequent interest payments, in tax-advantaged accounts. Tax-efficient assets, such index funds or equities with long-term capital gains potential, may be kept in taxable brokerage accounts.

3. Tax-Efficient Fund Selection:

Choose tax-efficient mutual funds or exchange-traded funds (ETFs) for your taxable brokerage accounts. These funds tend to have lower turnover and produce fewer capital gains distributions, which might result in lesser taxable income for you.

4. Harvest Tax Losses:

Tax-loss harvesting is selling assets that have incurred losses to offset capital gains, minimizing your total tax bill. You may use these losses to offset profits in the same year or carry them forward to offset future gains.

5. Hold Investments Long-Term:

Long-term investments held for over a year qualify for reduced long-term capital gains tax rates. Holding assets for the long term might assist lessen the tax burden when you ultimately sell them.

6. Utilize Tax-Efficient Investment Vehicles:

Consider assets that provide tax benefits, such as municipal bonds, which may generate tax-free interest income at the federal or state level. Additionally, certain assets, including eligible dividends or capital gains from stocks, may obtain favorable tax treatment.

7. Minimize Short-Term Capital Gains:

Short-term capital gains are often taxed at greater rates than long-term profits. To reduce short-term profits, be careful with frequent purchasing and selling of assets, since these activities might cause short-term capital gains.*8. Tax-Efficient Withdrawal Strategies:

When you begin taking money from your retirement accounts, carefully arrange your withdrawals to minimize taxes. Strategies may include minimizing your taxable income to keep inside particular tax rates or synchronizing withdrawals from several kinds of retirement funds to enhance tax efficiency.

9. Stay Informed About Tax Laws:

Tax rules and regulations vary throughout time. Stay updated about any modifications that may effect your investing plan. Consult with a tax counselor or financial expert to ensure you are taking advantage of all possible tax-efficient investing opportunities.

10. Consider Charitable Giving:

If you are tempted to make charitable gifts, research tax-efficient options to donate. Strategies like gifting valued stocks might give a tax benefit while avoiding capital gains taxes on the appreciated assets.

Tax-efficient investing is a vital component of improving your total investment results. By being proactive in managing your assets with taxes in mind, you may possibly minimize your tax bill and preserve more of your investment profits. Remember that tax regulations may be complicated, and individual situations vary, so it's essential to get expert guidance to establish a tax-efficient investing plan customized to your personal position and objectives.

Tax Deductions and Credits

Tax deductions and credits are important instruments that may decrease your total tax bill, putting more money back in your pocket. Understanding the difference between deductions and credits and understanding how to take advantage of them may have a major influence on your financial well-being. In this part, we'll cover both tax deductions and tax credits and emphasize their relevance in your financial planning.

Tax Deductions:

Tax deductions are costs or contributions that you may reduce from your taxable income, thus decreasing the amount of income subject to taxes. Here are some popular tax deductions:

1) Standard Deduction: The standard deduction is a predefined amount specified by the IRS that you may deduct from your taxable income without submitting itemized deductions. The standard deduction amount changes based on your filing status.

2) Itemized Deductions: Itemizing deductions entails documenting individual costs, such as mortgage interest, state and local taxes, medical expenses, and charitable donations, on your tax return. If your itemized deductions surpass the standard deduction, you might save money on your taxes.

3) Student Loan Interest Deduction: If you're repaying student loans, you may be qualified to deduct the interest paid on those loans, up to a specific maximum.

4) Home Mortgage Interest Deduction: You may deduct the interest paid on eligible mortgage loans for your main property and, in certain situations, a second home.

5) Medical Expense Deduction: If your eligible medical costs surpass a specific percentage of your adjusted gross income (AGI), you may deduct the excess amount.

6) Charitable Contribution Deduction: Contributions to qualifying charitable organizations are deductible, providing you have adequate paperwork.

7) Educator Expense Deduction: Teachers and qualifying educators may deduct some out-of-pocket expenditures for school materials.

8) Business expenditures: If you're self-employed or have unreimbursed

business expenditures, you may be
entitled to deduct these expenses on your
tax return.

Tax Credits

Tax credits directly lower the amount of taxes you owe. They are typically more beneficial than deductions since they give a dollar-for-dollar decrease in your tax obligation. Here are some popular tax credits:

1) kid Tax Credit: Families with qualified children may claim a tax credit for each kid. The credit amount depends on criteria such as the child's age and income.

2) Earned Income Tax Credit (EITC): The EITC is a credit for low to moderate-income people and families. It may result in a big refund even if you owe little or no income tax.

3) Child and Dependent Care Credit: If you pay for daycare or dependent care to

allow you to work, you may be entitled for a credit based on a percentage of those expenditures.

4) Education Credits: The American Opportunity Credit and the Lifetime Learning Credit give tax benefits for qualified education costs.

5) Saver's Credit: The Saver's Credit compensates qualified persons who contribute to retirement accounts, such as IRAs and 401(k)s, by granting a tax credit for their contributions.

6) Residential Energy Credits: If you make suitable energy-efficient modifications to your house, you may be entitled for credits, such as the Residential Energy Efficient Property Credit.

7) Health Coverage Tax Credit: Certain persons who are qualified for Trade

Adjustment Assistance (TAA), Pension Benefit Guaranty Corporation (PBGC) payments, or certain Alternative Trade Adjustment Assistance (ATAA) payments may claim this credit to assist cover the cost of health insurance.

Taking advantage of tax deductions and credits may dramatically lower your tax obligation and perhaps lead to a greater tax refund. However, eligibility for certain deductions and credits may vary based on your financial circumstances, filing status, and other variables. It's crucial to be knowledgeable about any tax advantages, maintain comprehensive records of your spending, and speak with a tax expert or utilize tax preparation software to guarantee you optimize your tax savings while keeping compliance with tax rules and regulations.

Chapter 8: Estate Planning: <u>Preparing Your Estate</u>

Estate planning is a vital component of financial management that frequently gets forgotten. It entails making a plan for the distribution of your assets, properties, and belongings following your demise. Estate planning is not only for the rich; it's a process that helps people and families of all economic levels. In this chapter, we'll cover the significance of estate planning and strategies to help you prepare your estate.

1. Why Estate Planning Matters:

a) Asset Distribution: Estate planning enables you to decide how your assets will be dispersed among your heirs and beneficiaries. Without a detailed plan, state laws and courts may decide how your assets are split, which may not coincide with your preferences.

b) Minimizing Taxes: Proper estate planning may assist limit the tax responsibilities for your heirs, ensuring they get more of your assets.

c) Guardianship: If you have small children, estate planning enables you appoint a guardian who will care for them in the case of your dying.

d) Healthcare preferences: Estate planning may include healthcare directives that define your preferences for medical treatment, end-of-life care, and organ donation.

e) Avoiding Probate: Effective estate preparation may help your heirs avoid the expensive and time-consuming probate procedure, which can postpone asset distribution.

2. Steps to Prepare Your Estate:

a) Create a Will: A will is a legal document that states how your assets should be transferred after your death. It also permits you to choose an executor who will handle your estate's affairs.

b) Consider a Trust: Depending on your financial circumstances and aspirations, you may want to form a trust. Trusts may allow greater control over the transfer of assets, privacy, and possible tax advantages.

c) Beneficiary Designations: Review and amend beneficiary designations on bank accounts, insurance policies, and retirement funds to ensure they represent your current preferences.

d) Power of Attorney: Designate someone you trust as your power of attorney to make financial and legal decisions on your behalf if you become incapacitated.

e) Advance Healthcare Directive: Prepare a healthcare directive (living will) that states your choices for medical treatment and designates a healthcare proxy to make decisions if you cannot.

f) Organize Your papers: Create a detailed inventory of your assets, debts, bank accounts, and vital papers. Share this information with your executor or a trusted family member.

g) Life Insurance: Assess your life insurance policy to guarantee it fulfills your family's financial requirements in the case of your demise.

h) Funeral and Burial Plans: Consider pre-planning your funeral and burial arrangements to reduce the load on your loved ones during a tough time.

I) Regular Updates: Review and revise your estate plan regularly, particularly following significant life events such as marriage, divorce, the birth of children, or changes in financial circumstances.

3. Professional Guidance:

While some people choose for DIY estate planning, it's typically best to seek expert counsel. An estate planning attorney may assist you manage the complexity of estate law, ensuring your paperwork are legally sound, and give useful insights customized to your individual circumstances.

4. Open Communication:

Discuss your estate plan with your loved ones, including beneficiaries and possible heirs. Clear communication may help avert misunderstandings and disputes later on.

5. Consider Charitable Giving:

Estate planning also gives chances to leave a legacy via charity contributions. You may select charity gifts or create a charitable foundation as part of your estate plan.

Estate planning is a careful and sensitive strategy to guarantee your desires are fulfilled, your loved ones are cared for, and your financial legacy continues. By taking proactive actions to plan your estate, you may give peace of mind for yourself and your family, even when you are no longer available to lead them.

Legacy and Charitable Giving

Creating a legacy via charitable giving is a meaningful approach to have a positive effect on issues and organizations that important to you. While it entails contributing a part of your assets or income to fund philanthropic initiatives, it also leaves a permanent impression that represents your values and views. In this section, we'll discuss the topic of legacy and charity giving, stressing its relevance and offering advise on how to make charitable donations a part of your financial strategy.

Why Legacy and Charitable Giving Matters:

1) Making a Difference: Charitable giving enables you to donate to issues you are

passionate about, whether it's helping education, healthcare, environmental protection, poverty reduction, or any other area of interest. Your gifts may have a real effect on these efforts.

2) Leaving a Legacy: Charitable giving is a method to leave a good legacy that goes beyond your lifetime. It gives a chance to create the world according to your ideas, goals, and vision.

3) Tax advantages: In many countries, including the United States, charitable gifts may result in tax advantages. You may be qualified for deductions or credits that lower your total tax obligation.

4) Community participation: Charitable giving develops a feeling of community participation and social responsibility. It encourages people and families to be

actively engaged in tackling society concerns.

Steps to Incorporate Charitable Giving into Your Financial Plan

a) Identify Your Passions: Determine the issues or organizations that connect most with you. Consider your own beliefs and the topics that matter significantly to you and your family.

b) Set Giving objectives: Establish clear giving objectives, both in terms of the amount you wish to donate and the effect you expect to accomplish via your gifts.

c) Create a Giving strategy: Develop a strategic giving strategy that describes how, when, and where you intend to make charitable donations. Consider setting up a specific charity giving budget.

d) investigate Charities: Thoroughly investigate charities and non-profit organizations to ensure they correspond with your ideals and function properly. Verify their openness, financial responsibility, and effect.

e) Explore Different Giving Vehicles: Charitable giving may take numerous forms, such as one-time gifts, regular contributions, donor-advised funds, or creating a charitable foundation. Choose the strategy that best matches your aims.

f) Maximize Tax advantages: Consult with a tax expert to understand the tax advantages connected with your charitable donation. Ensure you retain thorough records of your donations for tax reasons.

g) Engage Family: If you have a family, engage them in the charity giving process. Discuss your charitable aims with your loved ones and invite them to participate in the decision-making.

h) Leave a Legacy: Consider adding charity giving into your estate plan to guarantee your legacy of giving continues after your lifetime. You may designate charity organizations as beneficiaries in your will, trust, or retirement savings.

I) Stay Informed: Continuously educate yourself about charity giving opportunities, new philanthropic trends, and the effect of your gifts. Networking with other donors and philanthropists might bring helpful insights.

j) Evaluate and Adjust: Periodically examine the efficacy of your philanthropic contributions. Make modifications to your donating approach as required to optimize your effect.

Remember that charity giving is a personal and customized activity. There is no one-size-fits-all approach, and your giving strategy should reflect your individual circumstances and ideals. Whether you choose to support local groups, international issues, or a mix of both, your legacy of giving may produce a lasting, beneficial influence on the globe and the people you care about.

Part IV: Wealth Protection
Chapter 9: Risk Management and Insurance

Types of Insurance Coverage

Insurance is a critical component of a complete financial strategy. It offers protection against numerous dangers and unforeseen occurrences that might disturb your financial well-being. In this chapter, we'll review the numerous forms of insurance coverage accessible to people and families, helping you understand how each type might secure your financial stability.

1. Health Insurance:

Health insurance is vital for paying medical expenditures, including doctor's visits, hospital stays, prescription drugs, and preventative care. It guarantees you have access to vital healthcare treatments without incurring hefty out-of-pocket payments.

• Dental and Vision Insurance: These insurance offer coverage for dental and vision care treatments, including regular check-ups, cleanings, eyeglasses, and contact lenses.

2. Life Insurance:

Life insurance offers financial security for your loved ones in the case of your death. It pays out a death benefit to beneficiaries, helping them meet living costs, debt, and other financial commitments.

a) duration Life Insurance: Offers coverage for a specific duration, such as 10, 20, or 30 years. It's often more cheap but does not build financial worth.

b) Whole Life Insurance: Provides everlasting coverage and includes a cash value component that may increase over time. Premiums are often greater than term life insurance.

3. Disability Insurance:

Disability insurance covers a part of your income if you become disabled and unable to work. It assures you can maintain your level of life and meet everyday expenditures throughout a disability.

a) Short-Term Disability: Provides benefits for a short time, generally up to six months.

b) Long-Term Disability: Offers coverage for a lengthy term, perhaps until retirement age.

4. Auto Insurance:

Auto insurance is necessary in most countries and offers coverage in case of accidents, damage to your vehicle, responsibility for injuries or property damage to others, and theft.

a) Liability Insurance: Covers damages to others if you're at fault in an accident.

b) Collision Coverage: Pays for repairs or replacement of your car in case of an accident.

c) Comprehensive Coverage: Protects against non collision incidents including theft, vandalism, or natural catastrophes.

5. Homeowners or Renters Insurance:

Homeowners insurance offers coverage for your house and personal items in case of damage, theft, or liability claims.

Renters insurance gives comparable protection for renters, including personal property and liability.

6. Umbrella Insurance:

Umbrella insurance offers extra liability coverage beyond what is supplied by your vehicle, homeowners, or renters insurance. It is meant to shield you against huge lawsuits or liability claims.

7. Long-Term Care Insurance:

Long-term care insurance covers the expenses of extended care services, such as nursing home care, in-home care, or assisted living facilities, which are not normally covered by health insurance.

8. Travel Insurance:

Travel insurance offers coverage for trip cancellations, interruptions, medical crises overseas, lost luggage, and other travel-related disasters.

9. Pet Insurance:

Pet insurance helps cover veterinarian expenditures for your pets, ensuring they get critical medical care without incurring financial pressure.

10. Business Insurance:

Business insurance provides security for companies and their assets. It might include general liability, property insurance, workers' compensation, and more, depending on the unique requirements of the firm.

The sorts of insurance coverage you need will depend on your specific circumstances, financial objectives, and risk tolerance. It's vital to check your insurance requirements often and alter your coverage as required to ensure you are sufficiently covered against any threats. Consulting with an insurance specialist may help you make educated choices and pick the correct insurance plans to secure your financial stability.

Chapter 10: Financial Security for Life

Building a Financial Safety Net

A comprehensive financial safety net is the basis of financial stability, providing you with peace of mind and the capacity to weather unanticipated storms. In this chapter, we'll cover the fundamental components of a financial safety net and how to design one that protects your financial stability throughout life.

1. Emergency Fund:

Importance: An emergency fund is your first line of defense against unforeseen financial setbacks, such as medical problems, auto repairs, or job loss. It helps you avoid delving into your funds or getting into debt when life throws you a curveball.

a) Guidelines: Aim to save three to six months' worth of necessary living expenditures in your emergency fund. If you have a significant degree of employment insecurity or changeable income, consider saving even more.

b) Accessibility: Keep your emergency fund in a highly liquid and readily accessible account, such as a savings account or money market account.

2. Insurance Coverage:

a) Health Insurance: Ensure you have adequate health insurance coverage to guard against medical bills and unforeseen health difficulties.

b) vehicle and Home Insurance: Maintain vehicle and home insurance coverage to secure your property and assets from accidents, damage, or theft.

c) Life Insurance: If you have dependents or major financial responsibilities, consider life insurance to pay for your loved ones in case of your untimely death.

d) Disability Insurance: Protect your income with disability insurance, which offers financial help if you are unable to work due to disability.

e) Umbrella Insurance: For further liability protection, consider umbrella insurance to cover large-scale litigation or claims.

3. Debt Management:

a) Avoid High-Interest Debt: Minimize the use of high-interest credit cards and loans, since they may rapidly lead to financial hardship. Pay off high-interest debt as quickly as feasible.

b) Create a Debt Repayment Plan: Develop a plan to pay off current debts consistently. Focus on paying more than the minimum monthly payments to speed debt reduction.

4. Regular Budgeting:

a) Budgeting: Create and adhere to a monthly budget that records your income and spending. Regular budgeting helps you uncover areas where you may minimize expenditures and improve savings.

b) Emergency Budget: Develop an emergency budget that details critical

costs and discretionary spending you may
eliminate if required during financial
crisis.

5. Additional Savings:

a) Retirement Savings: Continue to
contribute to your retirement accounts,
such as 401(k)s and IRAs, to develop a
long-term financial safety net for your
retirement years.

b) Education and Investment Accounts:
Consider creating supplementary savings
or investment accounts for particular
aims, such as education financing or
wealth growth.

6. Legal and Estate Planning:

a) Wills and Trusts: Establish a will or trust
to guarantee your assets are transferred

according to your desires in the case of your dying.

b) Power of Attorney: Designate a trustworthy person to make financial and legal decisions on your behalf if you become incapacitated.

c) Advance Healthcare Directive: Prepare a healthcare directive (living will) to outline your medical treatment choices and select a healthcare proxy.

7. Regular Review:

a) Periodic Assessment: Regularly assess your financial safety net, insurance coverage, and savings objectives. Make modifications when your circumstances alter or grow.

Building a financial safety net is a continual process that demands discipline and careful preparation. While it may take time to completely develop, the peace of mind it brings is important. A solid financial safety net not only protects you from unanticipated financial shocks but also lays the basis for a lifetime of financial stability and well-being.

Financial Security for Life: Preparing for the Unexpected

Life is full of uncertainty, and financial stability is about more than simply acquiring money; it's also about being prepared for the unexpected. In this part, we'll study ways to reinforce your financial situation by taking efforts to prepare for unanticipated scenarios and crises.

1. Emergency Fund:

a) Foundation of Security: An emergency fund is your financial safety net. It's a pool of easily accessible cash that may cover critical living expenditures when unexpected circumstances occur.

b) Guidelines: Financial gurus frequently suggest accumulating three to six months' worth of living costs in your emergency fund. However, the optimal amount might vary according on your unique circumstances, employment stability, and risk tolerance.

c) Regular Contributions: Build your emergency fund gradually by putting away a percentage of your pay each month. Automate donations to guarantee consistency.

d) Emergency Use Only: Reserve your emergency money for actual emergencies, such as medical expenditures, auto repairs, or sudden job loss. Avoid utilizing it for frivolous expenditures.

2. Insurance Coverage:

a) Health Insurance: Adequate health insurance is necessary to defend against big medical expenditures and unforeseen health difficulties. Ensure you have comprehensive coverage for yourself and your family.

b) vehicle and Home Insurance: Maintain vehicle and home insurance coverage to secure your possessions from accidents, damage, or theft. Review and refresh your coverage frequently.

c) Life Insurance: If you have dependents or major financial responsibilities, consider life insurance to care for your loved ones in the case of your untimely death.

d) Disability Insurance: Protect your income with disability insurance, which gives financial help if you are unable to work due to disability.

3. Debt Management:

a) High-Interest Debt: High-interest credit card debt may swiftly destroy your financial stability. Prioritize paying off high-interest bills to alleviate financial stress.

b) Debt Repayment strategy: Develop an organized strategy for paying off current debts, emphasizing on paying more than the minimum monthly installments to speed the process.

4. Regular Budgeting:

a) Budget Creation: Establish and manage a monthly budget that records your revenue and spending. A budget helps you find areas where you may minimize expenditures and improve savings.

b) Emergency Budget: Prepare an emergency budget that identifies critical costs and discretionary spending that may be cut during financial crises.

5. Legal and Estate Planning:

a) Wills and Trusts: Establish a will or trust to guarantee your assets are dispersed according to your intentions if anything happens to you.

b) Power of Attorney: Designate a trustworthy person to make financial and legal decisions on your behalf if you become incapacitated.

c) Advance Healthcare Directive: Prepare a healthcare directive (living will) to outline your medical treatment choices and select a healthcare proxy.

6. Regular Review
 Periodic Assessment: Regularly assess your financial safety net, insurance coverage, and savings objectives. Make modifications when your circumstances alter or grow.

Preparing for the unexpected is a core part of financial stability. While it may take time and discipline to develop a comprehensive safety net, the financial piece of mind it brings is unparalleled. By applying these tactics and constantly bolstering your financial situation, you

may handle life's difficulties with
confidence and resilience.

Part V: Living a Happy Wealthy Life

Chapter 11: Wealth and Happiness The Connection between Wealth and Well-being

The relationship between wealth and happiness is a topic that has intrigued philosophers, economists, and psychologists for centuries. Many people aspire to accumulate wealth in the belief that it will lead to greater happiness and well-being. In this chapter, we'll explore the complex connection between wealth and happiness and how you can navigate this relationship in your pursuit of a fulfilling life.

1. The Pursuit of Wealth:

a) Financial Goals: Accumulating wealth is often seen as a means to achieve various financial goals, such as homeownership, retirement security, and providing for loved ones.

b) Financial Security: Wealth can provide a sense of financial security and reduce anxiety about meeting basic needs and unexpected expenses.
Freedom of Choice: Wealth can offer greater freedom and flexibility in choosing how you live your life, including where you live, how you work, and how you spend your time.

2. The Limits of Wealth:

a) The Hedonic Treadmill: Research suggests that people quickly adapt to increases in wealth and lifestyle improvements, returning to a baseline level of happiness over time. This phenomenon is known as the hedonic treadmill.

b) Materialism: Overemphasis on material possessions and the pursuit of wealth at the expense of other life aspects can lead to dissatisfaction and stress.

c) Diminishing Returns: Beyond a certain point, the marginal increase in happiness associated with accumulating more wealth becomes smaller, indicating diminishing returns.

<u>Balancing Wealth and Life</u>

Achieving a balance between wealth and life is a crucial aspect of overall well-being. While wealth can provide financial security and open doors to opportunities, it should not come at the expense of other essential elements of a fulfilling life.

 In this section, we'll explore the significance of balancing wealth with other aspects of life and offer guidance on how to achieve this equilibrium.

1. The Pursuit of Wealth:

a) Financial Goals: Accumulating wealth is often a key financial goal, as it enables you to achieve objectives such as homeownership, retirement security, and financial independence.

b) Security: Wealth can provide a sense of financial security, reducing stress and anxiety about meeting basic needs and unexpected expenses.

c) Freedom: Having financial resources can grant you greater freedom and flexibility in making life choices, including where you live, how you work, and how you spend your time.

2) Balancing Wealth with Life:

a) Define Your Values: Reflect on your core values and what truly matters to you in life. Understanding your values can guide your financial decisions and help you prioritize what brings you joy and fulfillment.

b) Set Boundaries: Establish boundaries between work and personal life. Avoid overextending yourself at work to the detriment of your health, relationships, and leisure time.

c) Mindful Spending: Practice mindful spending by allocating resources to experiences, relationships, and activities that genuinely enhance your well-being. Consider the value of experiences over material possessions.

d) Financial Planning: Engage in comprehensive financial planning to align your wealth-building efforts with your broader life goals and aspirations.

4. Non-Financial Sources of Happiness:

a) Relationships: Strong and supportive relationships with family and friends often play a more significant role in overall happiness than wealth.

b) Health: Good physical and mental health is a vital contributor to well-being and can't always be purchased with money.

c) Purpose and Fulfillment: Finding meaning and purpose in life, such as through meaningful work or contributing to the well-being of others, can be a more significant source of happiness than wealth alone.

5) The Pursuit of Well-being:
a) Well-being Strategies: Explore various well-being strategies, such as mindfulness, gratitude, and self-care, to enhance your happiness and life satisfaction.

b) Work-Life Balance: Prioritize a healthy work-life balance, as excessive focus on wealth accumulation can lead to burnout and decreased overall well-being.

c) Continuous Learning: Pursue personal and professional growth through continuous learning and self-improvement, which can contribute to a sense of purpose and fulfillment.

d) Balancing wealth and life is a dynamic and ongoing process. It involves continuously assessing your values, setting boundaries, and making conscious choices that align with your broader life goals. While financial security is essential, it should be a means to an end—supporting your pursuit of a well-rounded and fulfilling life that encompasses relationships, health, personal growth, and purpose. Ultimately, achieving this balance is a key component of lasting happiness and contentment.

Chapter 12: Giving Back and Philanthropy

The Joy of Giving

The act of giving back and engaging in philanthropy is not only a powerful force for positive change in the world but also a source of profound joy and fulfillment for individuals. In this chapter, we'll explore the intrinsic rewards of giving and the ways in which philanthropy can enrich your life.

1. The Joy of Generosity:

a) Intrinsic Satisfaction: Giving to others, whether through donations, volunteering, or acts of kindness, often brings an immediate sense of joy and satisfaction.

b) Positive Emotions: Generosity triggers the release of endorphins and activates brain regions associated with pleasure and reward, contributing to feelings of happiness and contentment.

c) Strengthening Relationships: Acts of giving can deepen relationships, fostering a sense of connectedness and belonging in your community and among friends and family.

2. The Impact of Philanthropy:

a) Creating Change: Philanthropy has the power to address pressing social issues, improve lives, and create positive change on a local, national, and global scale.

b) Sense of Purpose: Engaging in philanthropic activities provides a sense of purpose and meaning, allowing individuals to contribute to causes they are passionate about.

c) Legacy: Philanthropy allows you to leave a lasting legacy by supporting causes that align with your values and beliefs.

3) Ways to Experience the Joy of Giving:

a) Financial Donations: Contributing financially to charities, non-profit organizations, or causes you care about is a common and impactful way to give back.

b)Volunteering: Offering your time and skills through volunteer work can make a significant difference in your community and provide personal fulfillment.

c) Random Acts of Kindness: Simple acts of kindness, such as helping a neighbor, buying coffee for a stranger, or donating to a local food bank, can brighten someone's day and bring you joy.

d) Skills-Based Giving: Share your expertise and skills with organizations or individuals in need. For example, you can mentor, tutor, or provide pro bono services.

4. Philanthropy as a Lifelong Practice:

a) Regular Giving: Incorporate philanthropy into your life on an ongoing basis, rather than viewing it as a one-time event. Regular giving allows you to experience the joy of giving continuously.

b) Family Tradition: Teach the values of philanthropy to your family and involve your loved ones in charitable activities. Philanthropy can become a family tradition that fosters empathy and compassion.

c) Strategic Giving: Consider strategic philanthropy by aligning your giving with your passions and interests. Research and choose causes that resonate with you on a personal level.

d) Giving Circles: Join or form giving circles or philanthropic groups with like-minded individuals. Collective giving can amplify the impact of your contributions.

5. The Ripple Effect:

a) Inspiring Others: Your acts of generosity and philanthropy can inspire others to do the same, creating a ripple effect of positive change in your community and beyond.

b) Personal Growth: Engaging in philanthropy can lead to personal growth, increased empathy, and a deeper understanding of societal issues.

6) Reflecting on Your Impact:

a) Take Time to Reflect: Pause periodically to reflect on the impact of your philanthropic efforts and the joy it has brought you. Celebrate the positive change you've contributed to.

The joy of giving is a profound and enduring source of happiness. As you explore the world of philanthropy and engage in acts of generosity, you'll discover that the act of giving can be a deeply fulfilling and transformative experience. It not only benefits those in need but also enriches your life in ways that money alone cannot measure. Embracing the joy of giving can become an integral part of your journey toward a more meaningful and contented life.

b) Giving Back and Philanthropy: Making a Positive Impact

Philanthropy is a powerful force for positive change in the world, allowing individuals to contribute to causes they are passionate about and create a lasting impact on society.

In this section, we'll delve into the ways in which philanthropy can make a positive difference and inspire change, both on a personal level and within communities and beyond.

1. The Impact of Philanthropy:

Addressing Pressing Issues: Philanthropy enables individuals to actively engage in addressing critical social, environmental, and humanitarian issues. It can provide essential resources to tackle challenges such as poverty, hunger, disease, education disparities, and environmental conservation.

a) Transforming Lives: Through financial donations, volunteering, and support for non-profit organizations, philanthropy has the power to transform lives. It provides access to healthcare, education, clean water, and essential resources for those in need.

b) Building Stronger Communities: Philanthropic efforts strengthen communities by fostering a sense of unity and collaboration. When individuals come together to support a common cause, it leads to the development of stronger, more resilient communities.

2.Personal Fulfillment:

a) Sense of Purpose: Engaging in philanthropy can provide a deep sense of purpose and fulfillment. It allows individuals to align their actions with their values and contribute to causes that resonate with them personally.

b) Joy and Satisfaction: The act of giving, whether through financial contributions, volunteer work, or acts of kindness, often brings immediate joy and satisfaction. It activates brain regions associated with pleasure and reward, enhancing overall well-being.

c) Legacy and Meaning: Philanthropy allows individuals to leave a lasting legacy by supporting causes they believe in. It imparts meaning to one's life and ensures that their values and beliefs continue to make a positive impact even after they are gone.

3. Inspiring Change:

a) Setting an Example: Philanthropy sets an example for others to follow. When individuals lead by example and engage in giving back, it inspires those around them to do the same, creating a ripple effect of positive change.

b) Advocacy and Awareness: Philanthropists often become advocates for their chosen causes, raising awareness and mobilizing support to address pressing issues. They can influence policy changes and promote social justice.

4. Strategic Philanthropy:

a) Aligning Passions and Interests: Strategic philanthropy involves aligning your giving with your passions, interests, and areas of expertise. It allows you to make a more significant impact in areas that matter most to you.

b) Research and Due Diligence: Effective philanthropy involves researching and evaluating non-profit organizations and initiatives to ensure that your contributions are directed toward reputable and impactful projects.

c) Long-Term Commitment: Consider long-term commitments to causes and organizations. Sustainable change often requires ongoing support and dedication.

5. Collective Impact:

Collaborative Philanthropy: Joining or forming giving circles, philanthropic groups, or partnerships with like-minded individuals can amplify the impact of your contributions. Collective giving allows for larger-scale projects and greater influence.

Local and Global Reach: Philanthropy can have a local, national, or global reach. Whether you aim to support your immediate community or address global challenges, there are opportunities to make a difference.

6. Reflecting on Impact:

Regular Assessment: Periodically reflect on the impact of your philanthropic efforts. Celebrate the positive change you've contributed to and evaluate the effectiveness of your giving strategy.

Philanthropy is a dynamic and evolving journey that allows individuals to make a positive impact on the world while experiencing personal growth and fulfillment. By embracing the principles of giving back and engaging in philanthropy,

you can create a legacy of positive change
that extends far beyond your own life and
contributes to a better, more
compassionate world.

Conclusion: Your Journey to Financial Freedom

Congratulations on embarking on your journey to financial freedom! Throughout this book, "Discover the Pathway to Wealth: A Simple Guide to Financial Freedom and a Happy Life," you've explored a comprehensive roadmap to achieve financial security, wealth, and a fulfilling life.

 As you conclude this journey, it's essential to reflect on the key takeaways and the path ahead.

1. Defining Your Wealth Objectives: You've learned the importance of setting clear, specific, and achievable financial goals. By defining your wealth objectives, you've laid the foundation for your financial journey.

2. Understanding Money Psychology: Delving into the psychology of money has helped you uncover the emotional and behavioral factors that influence your financial decisions. Awareness of these factors empowers you to make more informed choices.

3. Building a Solid Financial Foundation: Establishing a budget, creating an emergency fund, and managing debt wisely are essential steps in building a robust financial foundation. These practices provide stability and security on your path to wealth.

4. Boosting Your Earning Potential: You've explored strategies for career advancement and diversifying your income streams. By actively working on increasing your earning potential, you're setting the stage for financial growth.

5. Investments and Wealth Growth: Understanding the basics of investing, diversifying your portfolio, and focusing on long-term wealth-building strategies are key components of accumulating wealth over time.

6. Retirement Planning: Recognizing the importance of retirement savings and exploring various retirement account options has set you on a path to secure your financial future.

7. Tax Strategies: Learning about tax-efficient investing, deductions, and credits has equipped you with knowledge to optimize your tax situation and keep more of your hard-earned money.

8. Estate Planning: Preparing your estate and considering legacy and charitable giving ensures that your financial legacy aligns with your values and supports causes you care about.

9. Risk Management and Insurance: You've explored the importance of various insurance types and strategies for protecting your wealth and well-being.

10. Financial Security for Life: Building a financial safety net ensures you're prepared for life's unexpected challenges, offering peace of mind and stability.

11. Wealth and Happiness: Understanding the complex relationship between wealth and happiness has helped you find a balance that prioritizes overall well-being.

12. Giving Back and Philanthropy: Engaging in philanthropy not only creates positive change in the world but also brings personal joy and fulfillment.

As you conclude this journey, remember that achieving financial freedom is not a destination but a continuous process. It requires ongoing learning, adaptability, and a commitment to your financial goals.

Embrace the joy of giving back, and consider how you can use your wealth to make a positive impact on your life and the lives of others.

Your journey to financial freedom is uniquely yours. It may involve challenges and setbacks, but with dedication, discipline, and the knowledge you've gained, you have the tools to overcome obstacles and move steadily toward your financial aspirations. Keep your values, passions, and well-being at the forefront of your financial decisions, and may your path to wealth be a fulfilling and joyful one.